Blogging for Money:
Myths and Mistakes to Avoid When Writing a Blog for Profit

Dr. Heidi Thorne, MBA/DBA

www.HeidiThorne.com

I0397510

wise relating to the Product, including, without limitation, any errors or omissions therein.

Table of Contents

About Heidi Thorne

INTRODUCTION: SAY WE'RE HAVING COFFEE AND YOU ASK ME ABOUT BLOGGING...

I've had a number of my offline networking friends ask me about blogging. *What does it take to be successful? Will I make any money? How should I use it for marketing?* They have a lot of questions. I did, too, in the beginning. Now, several years later, I've been through the trials and triumphs of writing a blog and using it for my business.

So let's pretend we're sharing a coffee and that you want to pick my brain about writing a blog. In the following pages, I'll share my experience with blogging for money and for marketing purposes. You'll get my insider's perspective on what works, what doesn't, and what you can expect (or not).

CHAPTER 1: WHY YOUR WHY WILL MAKE OR BREAK YOUR BLOG

Wondering how to start a blog? What comes as a surprise to many wannabe bloggers is that it has nothing to do with learning how to use WordPress or Blogger, or even knowing how to write. In fact, these are the last steps in the process. The absolute first thing that needs to be done is answer this important question:

Why do you want to have a blog?

The following answers are unacceptable:

I just want to tell everyone what I think (or know) about _____.

Everybody else has one.

I want to make a lot of easy money.

Why don't these work? Certainly, if you are blogging simply to express yourself or share your passions without any expectations for results, then your "why" doesn't matter. These are often called hobby blogs. What's interesting is that hobby bloggers can spend a massive amount of time and energy on these sites. But with no real objective other than to share, they can easily be disenchanted and quit due to the drain on their time and, sometimes, money.

Creating a "me too" blog because everyone has one will usually result in the blog being quickly abandoned because blog competition is fierce and it takes a significant investment of time, energy, and possibly money to make one a success.

And because the blogosphere is getting to be a very crowded space, the possibilities for making piles of easy cash from advertising and sponsorship revenues are slim.

So if you're expecting to build sales, web traffic, a fan base, a competitive edge, or a solid alternative income stream, your "why" is the first order of business for your blog.

Top 9 Reasons to Start a Blog

Here are some of the most productive reasons to start a blog, as well as some of the challenges that may be encountered:

1. *Sales.* While this is the ultimate goal for any business blogging efforts, to hope that a blog will easily and automatically convert web visitors into buyers is a stretch except for only the lowest investment products and services. "Selling" subscriptions to join an email list, download an eBook, or purchase some other low cost digital good are sales that a blog can easily convert.

2. *Demonstrate Expertise.* A blog can be a significant public relations venue where the blogger or company can showcase expertise or knowledge through what is written.

3. *Build an Email List.* By offering useful free (or even paid) content, bloggers can encourage people to join their marketing email lists. An email list of opt-in subscribers (who can be potential customers and fans!) can become one of the blog's key assets. Although excellent posts can often be enough to encourage subscriptions, usually some

3

other incentive, such as a free eBook or report, can sweeten the offer and encourage opt-ins.

IMPORTANT: When building an email list, NEVER, EVER use your personal email account to send broadcasts! Use a reputable email provider (e.g., MailChimp, AWeber, Constant Contact, etc.) to collect email addresses and send broadcasts. Also, consult an attorney about privacy policies you'll need to post on your blog when collecting personal information.

4. *Build a Fan Base.* Not all blog readers will become email subscribers or customers. Some are already overwhelmed with too much email. But these same folks may be interested in following a blogger on social media or through RSS type news feeds. This is another form of opting in and often may be a larger base than strictly email subscribers.

5. *Create an Additional Alternate Income Streams.* Blogs can create revenues from advertising or sponsorship sales, as well as product or service sales. Advertising revenues can be realized from the sale of banner or sidebar ads on the blogsite or from PPC (pay per click) type advertising (e.g., Google AdSense). However, "can" is the operative word here. There are no guarantees that a blog "will" create revenues now or in the future.

6. *News Feed.* A blog can become an official news channel which can be referenced by the public and the press. This can reduce the volume of press releases and media kits that need to be distributed.

7. *Educate Customers.* Some products and services may be difficult to purchase or use. A business blog can offer helpful information to facilitate the sale or help custom-

ers make the most of their purchase.

8. *Thought Leadership.* Just as with using a blog to demonstrate expertise, a blog can also be a platform for the posting and discussion of the blogger's mission, vision, or philosophy.

9. *Engage Audiences with Comments.* Some blogs are started to encourage comments from readers. The goal is to engage readers to establish a relationship with them or to gain valuable feedback. Unfortunately, two things often happen: 1) People are usually too busy to read AND leave a comment. 2) Those that do comment often have the ulterior motive of creating a backlink back to their own site. So they leave useless or self-serving comments that only waste time and resources to read and manage.

Why Your Why Isn't Enough

If you've figured out why you want to blog, congratulations! You're miles ahead of many people who start blogs without a solid purpose in mind. But that's just the first step. You need to figure out if your why is working... or not.

Here's a real life example. In early 2010, I started a blog on promotional giveaways and how to use them. Since there aren't too many blogs on this topic, it sounded like a great idea to encourage potential customers to buy from me because I was providing a value added service. So my "why" was to increase sales. My ideal sales funnel looked like this:

Read Blog > Visit My Promotional Shopsite > Buy!

About 45 percent of the traffic to my shopsite was from the blog. So it was working to a degree. It just wasn't converting. Here's what was likely happening:

Surf Web for Product Choices > Read My Blog (for clarification) > Visit My Promotional Shopsite (as suggested in blog post) > Buy from Competitor's Shopsite

I can only speculate, but my guess is that when visiting a competitor's shopsite, these folks had questions about confusing terms or products. They went to Google Search, typed in the phrase or topic in question, found my site, got the info, maybe looked at my shopsite, then bounced back to the initial shopsite(s) they were viewing.

How did I make this assumption? The organic search for my blog was 60 percent of the total traffic. Search keywords that people were using to find me were common promotional product terms, but very specific such as, "*6 oz. T-shirt.*" No promo buyers that I know ever enter that specific of a term. And the bounce rate was high, hovering near 80 percent. In essence, I was helping my competitors sell.

Granted, I could also observe that there were issues with my shopsite. But my guess is that it was an issue of price. The mega online promotional distributors could undercut me all day long. And web buyers are often bargain buyers.

So I changed my why to education and building an email list. If they bought from me, fine. If they didn't, I would have other things to sell to them which included my books and joining my email list. But even that wasn't enough of a why. Readers were enjoying the information, but weren't becoming "next step" buyers.

So four years later, I closed that blog. The investment was too high to maintain it in the form and function it had. I moved a lot of the content to a hosted site that still satisfies my whys of education and selling books, but also gave me a new why—and ROI—from advertising revenues.

If I wouldn't have known or questioned my why, I might still be spending a huge chunk of my life chasing an unrealistic goal. This also emphasizes the importance of understanding and analyzing a blog's web traffic (which we'll discuss later).

CHAPTER 2: FOCUS FAILURES

Trending now in the blogosphere: Unfocused Blog Syndrome, a malady that can plague newbie, frustrated, and burned out bloggers. Symptoms include:

• *A single blog with several widely divergent topic categories.* A single blog could have navigation links for categories as diverse as business, crafts, recipes, travel, raising kids, relationships, pop culture, health and nutrition, gardening, movies, self-improvement and more. I've even run across blogs with up to six or more distinct topics.

• *Sporadic blogging, usually hopping from topic to topic.* Why not? The blog has so many categories anyway! One day it's movies. The next day (or month) it's politics. Then we might see one of grandma's recipes two months later.

Sure, variety is welcome on ANY blog! So, yes, throw in a special off-topic post here and there to reveal human-ness, add a bit of variety, and create personal connections. But here's the downside: If a blog continually lacks clarity and cohesiveness, it makes it difficult to define the audience and to realize positive results.

What Causes Unfocused Blog Syndrome?

If, logically, bloggers—who can be expert writers and thinkers—know that chaotic blogging can be counter-productive and actually hurt a blog's performance, why do they succumb to this behavior? Common causes vary based on where they are in their blogging careers:

• *Newbies.* These enthusiastic folks are anxious to tell the world all about themselves, as well as what they think, and what they like. They erroneously reason that the more multifaceted they appear, the wider the appeal their blog will have.

• *Frustrated and Fried.* These folks may have been blogging for years and may be bored, frustrated, or burned out trying to come up with ideas for a blog whose topic may be limited or worn out.

• *Retired and Reborn Bloggers.* These folks may have blogged as part of another life or career. Like their "Frustrated and Fried" counterparts just discussed, they're tired of the topic(s) they've been required to address in the past. They may also be out of the business or community for which they blogged previously. They view this as their chance to set themselves free of any topic constraints and they're exploring ALL avenues.

Problems that Unfocused Blog Syndrome Causes

Here's what happens with an unfocused, chaotic blog:

• *Fragmented Appeal and Audience.* What is this blog about... really? Readers may be confused and wonder if there is enough reason for them to follow this blogger's work. It seeks to serve everyone and, in the process, serves no one.

• *Shifting Gears and Going Nowhere.* Mentally shifting gears from topic to topic can be time consuming and draining, causing bloggers to become frustrated and frazzled.

• *Juggling and Struggling.* In addition to the drain of shifting gears, pursuing multiple topic paths can be a huge time investment. That means the blogger has to continue to remain conversant in multiple topics as well. That takes research and engagement with the target community. Now multiply that by the number of topics. The result is a constant juggling of priorities and struggling to keep up with all of them.

Preventing Unfocused Blog Syndrome

So what can a blogger do to avoid falling into this blogging hole?

• *Narrow the Focus.* Narrow the focus of the blog to a couple primary topic categories OR a primary topic with relevant subtopics.

• *Know the Why.* Newbie bloggers may have heard that blogging is a cool thing to do. But they may not have a clear idea of why they should do this (or not!). Experienced, burned out bloggers may just want an escape from their previous blogging. Neither is a legitimate reason to make a significant investment of time and money (yes, blogging may have hard costs). There may be outlets other than blogging that could be a better fit for their creative energies and resources.

• *Assess the Topic's Depth.* Some topics are so limited that it's almost inevitable a blogger will lapse into exploring more and varied topics soon after launch. If a topic lacks enough depth to inspire, at minimum, a once a week post for years into the future, it may not have enough content fuel to keep going and should probably be abandoned in favor of a more expansive topic opportunity.

• *Find Other or Additional Writing Outlets.* Instead of

taking on the huge task of creating and maintaining a separate blog for less viable topics, explore others' blogs and websites that might be interested in hiring someone to write posts on these subjects. This can provide a lower investment outlet for varied creative energies.

CHAPTER 3: WHY NO ONE NEEDS YOUR BLOG

Before you launch your new blog, consider this: People are just overwhelmed by the sheer volume of information and entertainment now at their fingertips on phones, screens, and every imaginable device. Some call this information overload and information fatigue. But it's not just the volume of material out there; it's the pace and schedule at which it's being churned and spewed out.

Sure, you create good stuff. You may already write stellar thought provoking, entertaining, or helpful blog posts. However, writers and authors sometimes feel that if they make their work just a little bit better than someone else's, it will "cut through the clutter."

But here's the reality: You don't even know what "clutter" your audience may be dealing with. They've allowed in a confusing flurry of fluff and substance, often filtered by how they felt at the moment they encountered it. Not only will you have difficulty determining how your audience parses the information that comes their way, but where it ends up on their mental landscape is also in a constant state of flux.

Plus, whether due to overload or concern with privacy, many people are opting out or not opting in to receive alerts and communications from blogs, businesses, and social media.

Welcome to the attention deficit society.

So what shred of hope do you have to connect with people that matter (like blog readers!)? Is the answer Internet advertising (which is a hard dollar cost)? Or jumping on the hot social media platform *du jour*?

While, yes, these tactics may be helpful in reaching readers for whatever you offer, pursuing inbound marketing strategies should be at the heart of your blog promotion arsenal.

Offer Content Like It Was Church

At the risk of sounding crass or irreverent, your content should be religiously offered as if it was a Sunday (or whatever day is your sabbath) worship service. Why?

• *People come to expect, even anticipate, these events. You become part of their calendar, part of their mental landscape.*

• *When people come to expect something from you—and you deliver as expected and anticipated!—you build trust.*

• *People follow and buy from people they trust.*

I've had two super successful content "gods" that lead the way for me. I can almost set my clock on Tuesday and Thursday mornings by the informative and engaging emails I get from them.

How does their example combat information fatigue and overload? I know that, with rare exception for maybe a special announcement, these role models will only connect with me at a specified and limited time. I know my email inbox won't be overflowing with daily drivel from them all week and weekend long. Call it rules of engagement. That's respectful and successful. And it doesn't go unnoticed.

The Content Vending Machine

Switching gears from the divine to the mundane, your content should also be available when and where your followers want it and are most likely to engage with it... like a vending machine. Taking the vending machine concept a bit further, these days, your followers are "consumers," often "snacking" on bits and pieces of content instead of a whole serving. People want to be able to throw in their payment (be it actual dollars, becoming an email subscriber, or just giving their attention) and—boom!—content comes out.

For more informative content, the ultimate "vending machine" is Google and its search engine brethren. For more creative and literary work, that means being found in online communities, websites and networks of folks who gobble up your particular brand of blog.

In my book, *Business Competitive Advantage: A Handbook for Small Business Owners, Entrepreneurs and Consultants*, I stress that there are three "Fs" to build sales: You need to become "Friended, Famous and Found." That's how you get loaded into the content vending machine.

How Much Information is Too Much?

As discussed above, having a regular posting, email broadcast, or distribution schedule for your content, as well as availability and the ability to be found, can help your target audience avoid the effects of information overload and fatigue.

But let's take a look at the content itself. What works in terms of the time it will take to consume your blog posts, podcasts and videos?

Over the past couple of years with the rise of YouTube, I've seen a number of social media types suggesting that video is hot and should be part of every blogger's (vloggers?) arsenal. I agree with them in two respects. One, YouTube is one of the biggest search engines and is in the same conversation with its Google family. Two, it can make you appear more human, authentic and approachable.

But here's where I diverge from the "video is hot" theory. Video takes time to consume! In fact, I find myself bouncing out of sites that only offer content in video, or even audio, format. I read fast. REALLY fast. So, for me, give me the text! I can whiz through a blog post in sometimes a minute or less. If I have to slog through a five-minute video or—ugh!—30-minute audio blog, you've lost me. Plus, when I have gotten sucked into a video (or videos), I realize I've just wasted several minutes of my day because getting through mountains of reading in a reasonable time is a priority—make that necessity—for what I do (which is nonfiction book editing).

Everyone is different and some of your audience may want a variety of formats from text to audio to video. Here's what to consider:

• *Offer your content in multiple formats.* This requires extra work, but allows your audience to consume it in a way that makes sense for them.

• *Think content "snacking."* Shorter installments of your content can work for the attention starved and overwhelmed. You may have to experiment with various lengths of content to determine what works for your tribe.

CHAPTER 4: TO SELF HOST OR NOT TO SELF HOST YOUR BLOG? (AND HOW THAT DECISION AFFECTS YOUR BLOG INCOME)

One of the issues that confuses many new bloggers is hosting. Some don't realize what their options are. Due to their lack of knowledge, some newbies make poor decisions about where their blogs will be hosted—in other words, living!—on the Internet which can impact their blogging income.

What is a Hosted Blog?

A hosted blog is a blog site that is technically owned by someone other than the blogger. The host blog will house the blogs of many writers, although the level of separateness from the host will vary.

In some cases, the blog is a standalone site that is merely supported by the host. Examples of these sites would be a WordPress.com blog (not to be confused with WordPress.org which will be discussed later) and Blogger.

In other cases, the blog is part of a larger overall blog site, with the blogger's work being housed inside it. HubPages.com is an example of this type of site. On it, bloggers have an individual profile page, but all posts and articles are part of a larger whole.

PROS

Lower Cost. Usually the host site absorbs many, if not all, of the costs of hosting and maintenance for its bloggers. This is offered in exchange for the blogger's participation and content which can attract web traffic. The host site avoids having to pay for content development and can realize advertising revenues from ads hosted on site.

Potential for Share of Advertising Revenues. Some hosted blog sites offer a share of advertising revenues to their bloggers, others don't. For those that do, splits of revenues vary from site to site.

Lower Learning Curve for Managing Content. Usually these host sites offer a variety of content creation and management tools that are easy to learn and use. This helps the host by facilitating the development of quality content which, in turn, facilitates greater advertising revenues for themselves.

Traffic Analysis May be Shared. Blogs live and die by the traffic and advertising revenues they generate. So hosts collect a lot of data on the blogs and bloggers they support. Sometimes hosts share some (but maybe not all) data on traffic patterns, keywords, and search analysis with their bloggers. But they are not required to share this information and bloggers may need to do their own analyses.

CONS

No Separate Identity. On hosted blog sites, the name of the blogger or the blog is appended to the name of the host. For example, [blog name].wordpress.com. This is awkward for marketing purposes. A workaround that many bloggers use is to purchase a unique domain name and simply forward the domain to their hosted blog URL. However, this increases costs.

Low Level of Control. Bloggers may have little control over the structure and appearance of their hosted blogs. Worse is that it is also possible that a hosted site could close, leaving bloggers' content in limbo or loss.

Moving Content May be Difficult to Impossible and Time Consuming. If a hosted blogger decides he wants more control over his blog's fate, he may choose to move his hosted content over to a self hosted site. First issue he'll face is that the existing fans may not realize the blog has moved and he will lose followers (another reason why some bloggers choose to purchase a unique domain name and URL which forwards to the blog's hosted "home" on the web). Some hosts may even prohibit that action altogether since they assume ownership of the blog content. ALWAYS CHECK THE HOST SITE'S TERMS OF SERVICE FOR COPYRIGHT OWNERSHIP BEFORE SIGNING ON!

No Control Over Advertising Content or Revenue. Bloggers on hosted sites have no control over what ads are shown on their profiles or posts. Ads that are not appropriate or those of competitors could be shown. As well, the host site may determine when—and if!—ads will be shown which can affect bloggers' income from any shared advertising revenues.

Inability to Contract with Advertisers. The blogger is typically prohibited from running their own advertising (such as Google AdSense) on the host site, and even may be very limited in terms of what self promotion is allowed.

Businesses May Be Prohibited from Using Hosted Sites.

Some hosted blog sites prohibit use of their services by for-profit businesses, including for-profit blogging. They reason that a business can generate their own revenue and shouldn't need support for their content marketing efforts. Check the host site's terms of service to verify prohibited uses.

BOTTOM LINE: If you are blogging for the sole purpose of making money, a hosted blog is probably not for you!

What is a Self-Hosted Blog?

As the name implies, a self hosted blog is hosted by the blogger himself (or herself). This means that he will assume all costs and risks associated with hosting and maintaining it.

Self hosted blogs may use one of the popular blog platforms such as WordPress.org, Drupal, and Joomla. These platforms merely provide the software for the site's structure and content development functions. Platforms such as WordPress are "open source," meaning that they are built with the collaboration of many developers on a free basis. But that may be all that is free since these platforms provide no hosting whatsoever. Hosting and domain names are purchased through Internet registrar and hosting companies (e.g., GoDaddy, Bluehost, etc.).

Once the basic platform software is loaded, all hosting, content development, management, and risk is the responsibility of the blogger. However, there are significant advantages of a self hosted blog.

PROS

Greater Control. Self hosted blogs are not subject to whims of host sites. Bloggers can control every aspect of the site including software, structure, look, domain name, content, and future!

Opportunity to Make an Income from Advertising and Sponsorships. Making money is why most bloggers start blogging in the first place! When the blogger controls the site, he can realize ALL of the revenues from advertising and sponsorships. As well, he can choose his own advertisers and sponsors.

Ownership. Except for the blogging software (such as WordPress, Drupal, etc.) used, the content of the blog is owned by the blogger to do with as he or she sees fit, including repurposing it into other works.

CONS

Higher Cost. The first cost a self hosted blog incurs is hosting the domain. In addition to the domain name registration, the blog hosting will also incur a cost. This can run into hundreds of dollars a year. And these costs will go on as long as the blog exists. If an outside contractor is hired to manage the blog, it can get even more expensive, sometimes into the hundreds or thousands of dollars each year. (Self hosted blog costs will be discussed in another chapter.)

Responsibility for Management Can Be Time Consuming. Maintaining the blog in terms of comments, plugins (enhancements to the blogging software), traffic analysis, advertising, content development... the list goes on and on. This can be costly in terms of time.

Which Hosting Option is Better?

Actually, both hosted and self hosted bloggers can be successful. It all depends on the goals of the individual blogger. Many "hobby" bloggers who are blogging for fun or to connect with other like-minded folks, may be more drawn to a hosted blog opportunity. Those that may be blogging as a business itself, or as part of an overall content marketing program, may be more inclined to use self hosting to have more control over the business aspects of the site. Plus, as discussed earlier, for-profit blogging may be prohibited on hosted blog sites.

One thing is for sure. Know the pros and cons of each option BEFORE signing on!

Why I Moved Back to a Hosted Blog... But Maybe Not Forever

I started my blogging career as many bloggers do on WordPress.com, the hosted version of WordPress. Since I wasn't too sure about this whole adventure, it provided an easy way to get started in the blogosphere at low cost. I actually liked it until blogging became more integral to my business goals of gaining revenues from advertising.

So I moved my blog over to the self hosted WordPress.org platform. I featured Google AdSense ads and blatantly promoted my promotions business since I now owned the right to do so! I also started an additional blog on a related marketing topic. After about four years, I closed both blogs. Costs to maintain, in both time and hard dollars, were not getting covered by the pittance in advertising revenues generated. Plus, my business focus had changed which made it counterproductive to continue.

What to do now? I still wanted to have a home for my blog content which was popular and getting web traffic. I saw a tweet about a hosted blog site where writers could maintain their copyrights to content, plus get a share of advertising revenues. So I moved my blogging operation there.

Of course, I had to rebuild traffic to any posts I republished on the new site. It has proved to be a good move that allowed me to connect with a new audience. Even though the advertising revenue isn't stellar, all the backend tech maintenance and cost is absorbed by the host site. So, except for my time to write posts (which I would have expended even if I kept my self hosted blog), my blog is in the black, instead of in the red.

But will I stay here for the rest of my blog career? I'm not sure. The host site could change or close, requiring me to again make a hosted or self hosted decision. Monitoring of my results, compared with my current business objectives, will be the key determining factor.

CHAPTER 5: WHAT IS THE COST OF A SELF HOSTED BLOG?

For those who wish to have more control and income from their blogs, a self hosted blog is essential. Though a self hosted blog may use a free popular blogging software platform such as WordPress.org or Drupal, decisions about the look, content, and advertising sponsors are completely the responsibility of the blogger... along with ALL the costs.

Here is a quick overview of costs. Cost examples offered are as of the date of this book's publication and may be higher or lower.

Domain Name and URL

One of the first decisions that needs to be made is what to name the blog. The name of the blog can then be purchased as a domain name URL (website address) through registrars such as GoDaddy. Some registrars offer a very cheap promotional price for the first year. Then the price goes up for the second and future years. **This cost will apply, year after year, as long as the blog is active!**

Bloggers can also choose to add domain privacy so that their home addresses and personal information are not revealed in an Internet WHOIS database lookup; see your registrar's website for availability and details.

Domain Name Registration: Expect at least $15/year or more + applicable taxes and fees

Domain Privacy (optional): Expect at least $10/year or more + applicable taxes and fees

Hosting

On a hosted blog, the host site pays for the server that houses the blog. But for a self hosted blog, the blogger assumes this cost. Hosting gives the blog's content and software a place to "live" on the Internet. Many registrars, such as GoDaddy and Bluehost, offer special hosting packages for blogs.

When selecting hosting, a decision needs to be made about *shared hosting* versus *dedicated hosting*. Shared means that you are sharing the server space with many other blogs and websites. This helps save on costs for everyone on that server. However, should one site on the server be infected with malware or get hacked, there is also a chance that every site on the server could suffer the same fate and even get blacklisted. Costs for dedicated hosting, where one site is the only site on a server, are much more expensive.

Hosting costs are monthly, but are often paid for in advance for the entire year. Month-to-month hosting may not even be allowed. But if it is, it will be expensive.

Security and encryption of data flowing between visitors and the site is also of great importance these days. Though it doesn't offer a complete security package, purchasing an SSL (Secure Socket Layer) certificate is highly recommended. With it, the sites URL web address will begin with https:// to show that it is a secured site. One more reason to add SSL? As of January 2017, Google was supposed to start marking non-SSL secured sites as non-secure which could turn off visitors.

Self Hosting of Blog: Expect at least $10/month or more for shared blog hosting + applicable taxes and fees, usually paid in advance for the entire coming 12-month period

SSL Certificate: Expect at least $70/year for minimum protection for one site + applicable taxes and fees, again usually paid in advance for the entire coming 12-month period

Blog Themes

Primarily on the WordPress platform, themes can be applied to the blog to make it look and display in a way that will be appropriate for the audience or device. When selecting a theme, it is important to evaluate the theme's *responsive design*, meaning that it will display and be usable on a variety of devices such as mobile phones and tablets, in addition to desktops and laptops.

Many themes on the WordPress.org platform are free, but may have a fee for upgraded features. Theme developers and designers may also solicit "tip jar" type donations to help fund maintenance and development of themes.

Tip: Always make sure your theme software is updated with the latest version. It should also be a theme that is compatible with the latest version of your blogging software (e.g., WordPress) and should be continually updated by the theme provider. Hackers have been known to exploit vulnerabilities in themes, especially old, never updated ones.

Themes: $0 and up/month + applicable taxes and fees

Plugins

What is a plugin? *Plugins* are bits of software that can be appended to the blogging software to do a variety of special functions. Examples would include image handling, security (highly recommended!), spam comment control (also recommended), contact forms, and much, MUCH more! These can greatly enhance the functionality of a blog.

Like themes, many software developers offer their WordPress plugins for free, but may charge for upgraded features. Some may ask for "tip jar" type donations to help defray the costs of development.

Tip: Make sure your plugins are constantly updated with the latest version. They should be compatible with the latest version of your blogging software (e.g., WordPress) and make sure your plugin providers are continually updating them. Hackers have been known to exploit vulnerabilities in plugins with some very nasty attacks that could shut a blog down, steal site or visitor information, and more. Yikes!

Plugins: $0 and up/month + applicable taxes and fees

Legal

Publishing a blog is a legal event and Internet law is getting ever more complex! Protect yourself! Consult an attorney about developing terms of service and disclaimer for your blog and its content, as well as a privacy policy describing how you use any personal information (such as email addresses) you collect from visitors.

Depending on the topic of your blog, your attorney may also suggest additional preventive measures to protect you from media liabilities.

Legal: Depends entirely on the attorney or legal service provider you use. However, you can expect to spend at least a couple hundred dollars up to thousands on this item, depending on your unique circumstances.

Images

Be very careful about images you use on your blog! Use only images that are royalty free and that you have specific written permission to use. Check the terms of service for any stock image site to make sure that the images you choose are safe to use. Even if you take your own photos, make sure you have property and model releases to use images of people, places, and property.

Images: $0 and up/per image OR per month subscription + applicable taxes and fees

Surprised?

Surprised at all the costs? I'm not surprised if you're surprised! And this is just a rundown of the bare minimum costs of self hosting a blog. Costs can escalate quickly as you add features and functions such as video, podcasting, email marketing, and more. And as costs escalate, profits plummet. So thoroughly research costs and hosting options, and compare them with potential revenues, before launching headlong into blogging.

CHAPTER 6: THE BLOGGING GREEN (OR GOLD!) IS IN EVERGREEN CONTENT

Just as the trees and shrubs for which it is named, evergreen content is information that can be fresh and relevant for long periods of time. Creating evergreen content can be a way to help secure a blog's future. Evergreen topics may benefit from improved search engine ranking (SEO) due to their continued relevance and reference value, especially if targeted keywords are included.

For example, some posts of mine have had measurable traffic for four years or more. That's an eternity in the blogosphere!

Examples of Evergreen Content (and What Isn't)

What makes content evergreen? Evergreen topics are those that people have been concerned about or interested in for many years, sometimes decades or even centuries. **While the topics listed here do have a long "shelf life," they do evolve over time and may require updating.**

Though not an exhaustive list, some examples of EVERGREEN content could include (in alphabetical, not necessarily popular, order):

• *Animals, Plants, Nature, Pets, and Gardening.*

• *Art, Music, and Movie Critique and History.*

• *Basic Business Skills, Principles, and Philosophy.*

• *Cooking Techniques, Tips, Recipes, and Ingredients.*

• *Crafting Techniques, Designs, and Projects.*

• *Fiction, Literature, and Poetry of All Types, and Critique of It.*

• *History, Historical Research, and Analysis.*

• *Life Skills and Relationships.*

• *Motivation and Inspiration.*

• *Religion, Philosophy, and Spirituality.*

• *Sports Techniques, Rules, and History.*

• *Travel Destinations and Landmarks.*

• *Writing Technique, Critique, and Reference Works.*

Topics that can have LIMITED LIFE include:

• *Celebrities.*

• *Computers and the Internet.*

• *Fashion and Beauty.*

• *Health, Medicine, and Fitness.*

• *News.*

• *Politics.*

• *Product Reviews.*

• *Science.*

• *Sports (current games and players).*

• *Technology of all kinds.*

Why do these topics have limited life? A good example

is health. Even though it has been a human concern for millennia and some principles (such as yoga or anatomy) are timeless and universal, attitudes and developments on health change so frequently that what might be considered healthy or safe practice today may become a health hazard or problem tomorrow. Scary territory indeed for any blog writer since it requires constant monitoring and updating, as well as disclaimers developed with the help of an attorney. **(Actually, disclaimers are recommended for ALL blogs of any topic!)**

The Problem with Product Reviews

A popular topic category for bloggers is product reviews. While these reviews may attract web traffic, advertising, and sponsors in the near term, they could have a short shelf life due to changes in the product, the market, and consumer appeal.

As a side note, product reviews also carry with them the burden of compliance with Federal Trade Commission (FTC) regulations about disclosure of any material connection between the manufacturer or supplier and the blogger. Material connection would be payments of any type including money, free products or services, or other privileges and perks. Visit FTC.gov or consult an attorney for current disclosure requirements that apply to product reviews, sponsorships, and endorsements.

When Evergreen Becomes "Nevergreen"

Even though many of the evergreen topics may be relevant year after year, individual topics or works within these areas may become irrelevant due to a variety of factors including:

• *Changes in Consumer Tastes.*

- *Technological Developments.*
- *Changes in Philosophical Thought and Ethics.*
- *Issue or Topic is No Longer Newsworthy.*
- *Law or Regulation Changes.*
- *Changes in Demographics.*

Luckily, flexible online blog and website platforms allow for easier updates of existing content.

Is Your Content Ready for Retirement?

Since I've been very active in the areas of social media and mobile marketing, a blog with tips for small business seemed like a natural fit. So I launched it.

Then, the world changed.

The FCC (Federal Communication Commission) rolled out new regulations governing how things needed to be handled in the mobile marketing arena. Was my content still relevant? The basic principles were rock solid and still would be helpful today. However, to keep the blog updated and compliant would have been a continuing nightmare. So I closed it.

Lessons learned? Carefully consider topics if going for evergreen relevance. Also monitor the topic's environment on a regular basis to determine if changes, or even retirement, is a prudent path.

How Evergreen are You?

Look over your blog post inventory and log how much is evergreen. Low percentage? Maybe that's why traffic and sales are low are dropping or non-existent. Might be time to rethink topics or the future of your blog.

CHAPTER 7: DON'T BE A PEST WHEN YOU GUEST BLOG

Guest blogging is writing or preparing content for a blog that is not owned or run by the writer. The advantage to the host blog is that by using guest bloggers, they can provide quality content at a much lower cost than by doing it themselves. For the blogger, it exposes their expertise and writing talent to a new audience and helps build an online reputation. Plus, guest bloggers benefit from backlinks to their own blog sites that may be included within the content, in a byline, or bio section.

But there are rules of etiquette and guest blogging tips that must be followed by both parties to make it a successful effort.

How to Become a Guest Blogger

Typical qualifications for becoming a guest blogger include:

• *Being a recognized expert on the host blog's subject area or industry.*

• *Portfolio of other published work in the subject area or industry.*

• *Website or a complete LinkedIn profile.*

• *Excellent writing skills in the language used on the blog.*

Notice that the last qualification is writing. Blogs don't need writers, they need experts! Proposing a guest post without being an expert will often meet with rejection since featuring unknowns doesn't help the blog site establish or maintain their competitive position as an authority.

That being said, there may be blogs who hire competent writers to develop content for them. When approaching a blog and its editor, be clear about the intent to write as an authority on the subject or as a writer for hire.

Becoming a guest blogger does not usually require a formal job application, although some blogs may have an extensive review process. Many blogs will publish guest blogging guidelines on their sites. Realize that even if those guidelines are followed, do not expect to be automatically accepted.

"Don't Call Us... We'll Call You"

Be aware that many blogs adopt a *"Don't Call Us... We'll Call You"* policy when it comes to guest bloggers. Why? They're not being rude. Blogs are highly protective of the content they're presenting to the world. Essentially, guest bloggers are squatters on their sites, using their Internet real estate.

Don't get offended! Get famous! Become such an expert in your field that blogs will call (or email) to invite you to post for them.

Guest Blogging Guidelines

Though guidelines can vary from one site to the other, there are some general rules of etiquette to follow to help score a guest blog placement:

1. *Understand that the blog is making an investment.*

Blogs need to allot file storage space on their sites for guest posts. As well, they need to maintain and promote the sites and posts, both of which cost money. Guest writers are getting to use those services for free.

2. *Blogs usually have excellent writers on staff.* With the possible exception of small businesses that may be short staffed, blogs are usually started by writers and companies that already have skilled writers on staff. They don't need another writer on board.

3. *Blogs are under no obligation to accept any guest post.* Some writers get dejected or even angry when a blog rejects a guest proposal or post. A blog is not a charity! It's a business.

4. *Pay attention to SEO.* Blogs post to build their placement on Google and other search engines. To ignore target keywords for the host blog's topic reduces the benefits of a guest post. As with all online writing, overstuffing a post with keywords will do more damage than good, eliminating any SEO benefit the site would have gained.

5. *Don't expect to be paid, but it is possible.* Some sites may pay for guest posts, but most don't. Usually, if a site is willing to pay for posts, it will recruit and pay writers of their choosing.

6. *Don't expect the blog to publish the post on a desired date.* A blog will include a guest post when it fits within the editorial calendar which could be months down the road. Hounding the blog to get a guest post published on a certain date will result in one thing: Rejection and removal from the publishing calendar.

7. *Treat a guest post request like a sales call.* Because it is! Be polite and respect the site's established protocol for

contact. Sell them on qualifications to write on the subject and what benefits they will gain from the relationship. Writers stand to get "paid" by gaining access to the site's audience.

8. *Properly attribute multimedia content provided.* If providing photos, graphics, videos, etc., also provide complete attribution and release information to protect everyone: Writer, multimedia creator, and the blog site owner. Realize, though, that blogs may wish to add their own properly licensed illustrations and multimedia elements.

9. *If employed, get employer approval before guesting.* Guest posting on a competitor's or other unapproved site could spell trouble for both employers and employees. If you're employed, get permission first!

10. *Don't over-guest.* Being a guest on every imaginable and relevant blog is not necessary and can waste valuable time and effort. Only pursue and accept guesting opportunities that meet sales or marketing goals. Also, accepting multiple free guest invitations from a single blog can quickly turn into a regular, but unpaid, writing assignment that can detract from pursuing paid business and opportunities. Other than occasional "freebies," it should be pay to play or walk away.

CHAPTER 8: WHY SUCCESSFUL BLOGGERS CAN BE THE WORST ROLE MODELS

As I look over the myriad of "how to blog" or "blogging success" books, I am floored by the number that claim a blogger can make up to thousands a month. These claims always cause me to ask, *"Why hasn't that happened for me?"* But just as I expect, these programs and strategies have some serious flaws, primary of which is the *"If it worked for me, it'll work for you"* fallacy. While learning from people who have "been there, done that" is valuable, watch for these errors in logic before investing in these programs and people.

Blogging Myths and Unicorns

"In 2001, I started my blog and have been successful ever since."

Look at the year. That was a long time ago. That was before the economic fallout from the 9/11 attacks, the recession of 2008, and the explosion of millions and millions and millions of blogs. There are 75 million blogs just on WordPress alone as of this writing according to Word-Press.org... and that doesn't include blogs on other platforms such as Blogger, Drupal, Joomla, and others. Though determining the exact number of blogs in the world is difficult, I've seen rough estimates as high as 150 million or more.

Also, wild success may have been realized by early adopters in the blogging arena. In addition to the impact of right timing, those who have been in a market longest often make more money than later entrants.

For example, I can boast that I made tens of thousands of dollars over the years through connections I made on Twitter, the microblogging platform. But is my result duplicatable? No! Twitter, my business focus, and my audience have changed dramatically since I got on board in late 2008. Twitter no longer works the same way for me. I would have an integrity crisis if I tried to tell people that what I did would work for them now, if at all.

Blogging Myth Blown: What worked "back in the day," may not work now.

"How I used guest blogging (or social media) to get 10K new email blog subscribers."

Guest blogging is a good thing. Social media is a good thing. Sometimes, though, blog success programs boast that they are surefire good things.

Blogging Myth Blown: Results from guest blogging or social media efforts may have been achieved many years ago, prior to the blog explosion and extreme information overload that is only getting worse. It is very difficult to get people to opt in to email these days, even with excellent incentives. There's just too much good stuff out there.

It's been my experience that these results are fleeting. Today's hot post will be lost in what's trending tomorrow. As well, I've found that visitors to the guest blog post can assume that the post was done by the host blog owners or staff, lowering the chances of visitor click through to the guest blogger's site.

Also, is this result duplicatable? It might be easy to get one big hit or rush of blog success. But can another big one be obtained in the second month? Every month? I want continuing results, not a one-hit wonder. Also, if the strategies only work in specific situations, these results are not duplicatable.

"You may need to invest in additional products and services."

My favorite was the webinar where a participant asked what other investments would be required to achieve success with the promoted program. Then the laundry list of Facebook ads, email automation, and other purchases came out... which, of course, added hundreds, if not thousands, of dollars on top of the coaching program cost.

Blogging Myth Blown: Information or educational content merely points the way. Investments in products, services, and time will almost always be required to be successful. But be careful if those aspects of the program or strategy are glossed over or completely missing. Get all the facts before investing.

"Make hundreds (thousands?) from affiliate income on your blog."

One of the more popular ways that blogs make money is through affiliate programs. What is an affiliate program? A seller of a product or service will pay a blogger or influencer a commission on any sales the blogger helps generate through his blog and/or through email and social media marketing. Usually, this is done through a special affiliate link included in a post or email, sometimes with a product ad on the blog. That link triggers tracking of the clicks and sales so that the seller can pay the blogger a commission when the sale is complete. These programs are often facilitated through an online service that connects the seller and the blogger affiliate.

In theory, these programs are fantastic and worth considering. However, there are some caveats.

Blogging Myth Blown: Though I have made a little bit of money with them, affiliate programs are not always a slam dunk income opportunity because:

1. *They're sometimes more hassle than they're worth.* I've sometimes spent hours copying links and posting them on my sites, on social media, or email, with little to show for it.

2. *Some of the products available in these programs seem scammy.* Some affiliate products can be so outrageous that I would feel icky promoting them. Remember, this is your blog space and scams could brand you in the same light. Choose affiliate programs with caution. These days I usually only consider those opportunities that are offered by people I know and trust to do right by my blog readers and email subscribers.

3. *It takes time to sift through the various opportunities.* On sites where there's a "marketplace" of sorts to connect sellers and bloggers, there could be hundreds, if not thousands, of opportunities available. Sifting through them and then having to evaluate each for relevance and trustworthiness can be very time consuming. Now I save my time by only considering programs that are offered by those I can trust.

4. *Blog visitors don't automatically or frequently click and buy.* Blog visitors can be turned off by product display ads since they're usually visiting for information, not to purchase. Some may even have ad blockers enabled. The trend toward ad blocking will continue to be one to watch.

5. *It's easy to overdo it on the affiliate marketing, especially with email.* I can almost guarantee that I'll get one or two of these third-party affiliate marketing pitches per week from a couple of bloggers I follow. Blog subscribers can get annoyed and either ignore these pitches or, worse, unsubscribe.

Carefully evaluate affiliate programs in terms of the time and effort required and the potential for annoying your blog subscribers and visitors. Also, only pitch those affiliate programs that have relevance for your audience.

Also remember that any "material" connection you have to affiliate sellers—meaning you receive some form of payment in cash, products, perks, promotional consideration, or anything else!—must be disclosed when promoting these third-party products and offerings. For rules on advertising, influencer, and endorsement disclosure requirements, visit FTC.gov (in the U.S.) or the government agency in your country that oversees these issues.

Questions to Ask BEFORE You Launch Any Blog "Success" Strategy

Although I approach these success strategies with a healthy dose of skepticism, I will admit that I have gotten some excellent ideas that were buried beneath the bull. So when I evaluate any of them, here are questions I ask myself:

1. *What unique circumstances could have contributed to the*

reported success?

2. When were the results achieved?

3. Can these results be duplicated across industries and circumstances? If not, where and when are these results most likely to be achieved?

4. What else would I need to be, do, have, or spend to achieve these results?

5. What qualifies this company or presenter to discuss this subject?

CHAPTER 9: MEASURING BLOG SUCCESS

What makes a blog a success? Traffic? Income? Interaction with readers? Personal satisfaction and expression? It could be any or all of the above. But measuring blogging success needs to be done based on some quantifiable factors.

Blogging Busy Work and Burnout

When some bloggers launch their sites, they also launch into hyperdrive. They try to blog every day. They reason, *"What's a little blog post gonna take to write? Twenty minutes?"*

In the beginning, a blogger may be able to hammer out a wave of posts in a hurry since the creativity cache is overflowing with ideas. Then, maybe six months in, the cache dries up. It gets harder and harder to come up with new ideas. A post might take 20 hours to get done. Eventually, the posting stream turns into a trickle, maybe even down to nothing.

Contributing to the burnout is the fact that the blogger's work and life keep going on. Family and social obligations, keeping up with business activities, exercising, social media... the list goes on and on. Bloggers get exhausted trying to keep up with it all. Something's gotta give and usually it's the blog.

Then there are some bloggers that flip in the other direction. Instead of abandoning the blog, they make it their priority and neglect other work and life responsibilities. That might work if the blog is a roaring financial success, though that is rarely the case. The blog often becomes busy work that feels like real work, allowing the blogger to escape from more important personal and professional obligations.

Tips for Measuring Blog Success: If finding time to write and maintain a blog is extremely difficult, evaluate whether a reduction in posting frequency might make the blog more manageable. Also, be realistic in evaluating a blog's success. A blog can be a huge investment of time and money though it seems cheap in theory.

The Comment Conundrum

Blog comments are quite gratifying to bloggers. Aside from the stupid spam comments (which can be quite amusing to read!), insightful comments show that readers have taken their precious time to add to the conversation the blogger launched. That can help bloggers understand what issues and topics are resonating with their audiences, maybe even inspiring more blog post topics. It may also identify some potential clients or business partners since these folks have self-identified themselves as interested parties.

Or maybe not.

While certainly there are sincere commenters on the web, many people who comment—particularly on big, very popular blogs—are looking for the Internet gold of backlinks to their own sites. Backlinks from popular, authority or well trafficked sites can signal to search engines that a site is relevant or valuable. So unless a blogsite is structured to limit comments to only those from registered users or community members, the possibility exists for backlink squatters who comment just to gain from association with a popular site... or many sites of all types. Many of these "spammenters" (the combo of "spammer" and "commenter") can be quite audacious and include a link to their sites right within the comment.

The wave of spam comments that bloggers must contend with can also be generated by bots and questionable sources for the same backlink bounty. Sometimes clearing out the myriad of these junk comments can be a chore, increasing the operating cost (in time and money) to run the blog. Another factor that needs to be considered when assessing a blog's cost.

With the scarcity of genuine comments on many niche blogsites, bloggers can feel that they are failing which may, or may not, be true. Realize that readers are very, VERY overwhelmed and multitasked these days. So they may be reading blog posts, but may not comment even if they really agree or like the post. They're just too busy and distracted to take the time to comment.

Another metric which could be a bit more encouraging and useful is to monitor sharing of blog posts with readers' followers and communities on social media and elsewhere. Even if they don't have time to comment, readers may think enough of a post to share it on social media. That is a comment in and of itself! Actually, sharing can even be more helpful than comments since it can amplify the reach of the post and the blog.

Tips for Measuring Blog Success: Measuring blog success based on the number of comments can produced skewed and disheartening statistics, especially for smaller, niche blogs. So certainly measure them, but evaluate the results in light of the issues discussed here before changing or abandoning a blog effort. Also monitor post sharing statistics which can provide insight into what resonates with readers.

Blog Traffic Traps

A relevant blog can have tremendous power in building a community of followers and potential customers. But beware of these traffic traps when measuring a blog's success:

• *Impatience.* Building traffic through SEO (search engine optimization) techniques can take many months to produce results. Because many business folks are obsessed with results they can get NOW (or at least this quarter), they quickly abandon blog and content marketing strategies before they can even produce traffic.

• *Dead Ends.* Even if a blog can generate a groundswell of traffic, if readers are not taking a desired action such as visiting a specific website or making a purchase after reading, the blog can become a dead end. The blog will drain resources while producing nothing.

Determining the success of a blog, requires continual monitoring of traffic patterns both to and from the blog. If the purpose of the blog is purely recreational and conversational, this is less of an issue, although there are hobby bloggers who obsess over statistics. Set up Google Analytics (or other traffic monitoring system) for the blog. Monitor traffic regularly. Depending on the topic and objectives of the blog, monitoring intervals could be daily, weekly or monthly, in addition to an annual review.

Tips for Measuring Blog Success: Be cautious of over-reacting to minor or short-term fluctuations in traffic. Watch for trends over an extended period of time, such as a year. Comparing year-to-year traffic trends can be very helpful in determining if changes need to be made. In addition to raw traffic numbers, watching where the traffic is coming from can be incredibly useful since it will help determine if blog marketing and outreach efforts are successful.

How a Penguin, Panda, or Hummingbird Could Affect Your Blog Traffic and Income

The success of blogs that are informational depend on their ability to be found on search engines such as Google and Bing. Therefore, the artful and natural inclusion of SEO (search engine optimization) keywords could be critical to getting your blog and its posts found online. For example, around 59 percent of the traffic to my current blog is generated through organic search as of this writing.

But here's the catch. Google, one of the world's premier search engines, is continually updating their search procedures (algorithms). They do this to prevent scammers and spammers from gaming the system and to improve the user experience.

Even if your site and content are legit, it might still be affected. So the keywords, meta tags, etc. that may get you found today, may be completely different tomorrow. Some of the more significant Google updates have been given names such as Penguin, Panda, and Hummingbird. After these update events, it can take blogs and websites days, weeks, or even months to recover traffic and advertising income.

Tips for Measuring Blog Success: Don't panic! These algorithm updates will continue well into the foreseeable future. They can affect everyone, the good and the bad alike. Subscribe to news feeds and blogs that discuss the impact of search engine changes on SEO. That way you'll know when an update could be affecting your traffic.

Regardless of the search engine situation, well written, quality blog content will help improve your placement in search results in the long run.

Not Enough Eyeballs

Another reason why your blog traffic may be low is because there just aren't enough relevant eyeballs to read it. True, there are millions and millions of people on the web all around the world. But that doesn't mean they all are ideal readers for your work.

In business, a common axiom is that when you narrow your focus, you broaden your appeal to that market or audience. We already talked about the necessity of focusing your blog. However, there comes a point where the focus can be so narrow or targets such a small niche, that there is not enough critical mass to attract web traffic.

Yes, a case can be made for what are called "long-tail keyword" topics. These topics have low traffic, but possibly committed followers. That being said, the long tail can also mean a long time to realize results traffic-wise.

Tips for Measuring Blog Success: Even before you start a blog, evaluate search results numbers for your blog topic. You don't want to jump into a super highly competitive pool that already has millions and millions of search results. But if you type your topic into search and only a few results (low thousands), very old, or seemingly unrelated results appear when you type it into the Google search, those are signals that it might not be a topic with a significant pool of potential readers.

What about the Money?

Okay, this is what you're probably dying to know! How much can you make from your blog?

Of course, I have to tell you that blog income levels range from $0 to thousands per month. I will also tell you that blog incomes in my community of blogger friends can fluctuate dramatically over time, often in response to search engine algorithm updates.

As well, income levels vary widely from blogger to blogger, depending on the blogger's topic, experience level, market, and a myriad of other factors. Some in my blogging community have reported monthly earnings of $200 to $600. Others have reported that a few years ago they were making $500 a month and now it's down to about $50. As you can see, it's all over the income map.

So I cannot even venture to guess how much you will make from blogging. But one thing I can safely say is that expecting to replace your regular employment or business income from blogging may be unrealistic in the current blogging arena due to high competition from millions upon millions of blogs and every other conceivable content type (video, audio, gaming, etc.).

Then there's the question of what does "blog income" really mean. Blog related income can come from:

• *Ad revenue from PPC (Pay per Click) programs such as Google AdSense.*

• *Sale of your own information products (such as eBooks) or services sold through the blog site.*

• *Cash sponsorships for being an influencer.*

• *Commissions from sales of third-party affiliate products and services sold on and through the blogsite.*

• *Sales of other products and services (speaking, consulting, etc.) that result from someone reading the blog.*

• *All of the above?*

Note: Make sure you disclose any "material" connection to your advertising sponsors and blog income sources. The FTC and government agencies are watching! In the U.S., visit FTC.gov for endorsement requirements or consult an attorney.

For me, I've made more money *because* of my blogging, than *from* the blog itself. I've been able to use my blog material as the basis for books, eBooks, and presentations. As well, I was hired to write for a corporate blog for an extended period and got speaking engagements that included paid travel expenses. So while I monitor ad revenues, I look at what I've been able to accomplish because of this adventure.

Realize, also, that your mix of blog income streams may change over time in response to changes in the market, search engine algorithm updates, and new or vanishing opportunities. One of the big trends that could impact blog advertising income is the use of ad blockers by blog visitors. I think this is why we are seeing a rise in the use of influencer sponsorships.

Tips for Measuring Blog Success: Monitor each blog income stream (advertising and sponsorships, affiliate commissions, speaking, book sales, etc.) separately, as well as a collective total for all blog income streams, so you can see where changes are occurring. At least monthly monitoring is recommended to more easily identify trends throughout the year.

Don't forget that all blog income streams must be reported on your income tax returns. Also be aware that sales of products and services may require collection, reporting, and payment of sales taxes. Consult a CPA or tax advisor for guidance on all tax matters.

CHAPTER 10: CLOSING YOUR BLOG COULD BE THE BEST THING YOU COULD DO FOR IT (AND YOURSELF!)

Confession: I'm a blogger and I closed two blogs. What? Why would I do that, especially since the one had been going for a number of years and had decent traffic?

Here's another confession: It was a difficult decision. But weighing the costs and future potential of these two sites helped make this action a no-brainer.

It's easy to become so engrossed in creating and running a blog that signs indicating a poor outlook for its future are ignored. In the discussion below are questions to help gain an objective perspective on one's blogging activities.

How I Made My Blog Closing Decision

In my case, I had two blogs on different niche marketing topics. The second was actually a spinoff from the more established blog.

Actually, I closed the spinoff blog first. New regulations applying to this marketing niche would have required a complete overhaul of the blog's existing material. Ugh! Even doing a few cursory changes took a full day or two of time. As well, the new landscape for this niche was bound to continue to change as the new regulations became standard practice, meaning more and more updating. That, coupled with the fact that the blog had failed to attract a decent amount of opt-in email subscribers (translation: potential customers) in about two years, even with a variety of incentives, the decision was quick in coming.

But what to do about the larger blog that had been going for about four years? The topic was still relevant and had a decent amount of fans for this niche. But like the spinoff blog, it didn't create a reliable sales funnel of customers. A significant percentage of traffic to one of my shopsites was generated by the blog. Unfortunately, that was not the site where online sales were coming from! Visitors to the established blog were usually reading the articles and bouncing out... but not bouncing to buy. The majority of traffic to the shopsites was from organic search results.

There were several reasons which could have accounted for this blog visitor behavior. It appeared that visitors were seeking the educational material I offered, but then buying elsewhere (online or off). Many of my friendly competitors were also visiting fans. I don't have a problem with that since I feel we need to share our knowledge. But the bottom line is that they are not going to buy from me.

Because I realized that my blog was an educational site, I tried to monetize it with Google AdSense, sales of self-published books and other services. Book sales were okay, though not paying the mortgage. But AdSense was generating next to nothing, sometimes literally nothing. Got a few leads for services, but most wanted me to guest blog for free.

Looking at receiving almost no income or leads over an extended period of time, coupled with the costs to maintain the site, I decided to close this blogging chapter, too.

Weighing Blogging Costs and Benefits

Because a blog can be a very personal and emotional effort, bloggers can often become blind to the host of hard and soft costs that blogging can entail. What determines whether these costs are deal breakers is largely based on what are the objectives for pursuing this effort. Assessing the future market for the blog's topic and potential for generating sales is also critical. The following questions can help bring the issues into focus:

• *How much is it costing, in hard dollars, to maintain the blog?* A couple dollars a month for services such as email subscriber collection, spam protection, backup services, image licensing, domain registration, hosting and helpful software plugins may not seem like a lot. But adding it up over the course of a year can run into the hundreds, even thousands, of dollars. Do a profit and loss analysis! Granted, many bloggers use free platforms such as WordPress.com and Blogger which do not have some of these hard costs. But the next question will show how it can be costing a lot no matter what!

• *How much is it costing in time to maintain the blog?* This can be a difficult question to answer, especially for hobby bloggers who may not be blogging for bucks. But for those who are doing it as a business or to gain business, this can be a significant investment. Small business owners and freelancers who blog could be forfeiting income that could be gained from simply upping their sales efforts instead of blogging. Figuring an hourly rate of income will be very revealing in determining the labor cost associated with a blog. And that cost could be very high!

• *Are you suffering from burnout?* Blogging can be a job in itself! Trying to squeeze in writing a blog post or two in an already hectic lifestyle can be exhausting! And multitasking can make the blogger less effective in everything.

• *Is the blog generating income?* For hobby bloggers who are simply publishing to connect with like-minded individuals, income may be an afterthought. But for those who are blogging for money, income generated is a critical factor in a continue/close decision process. Even if it is generating income, is it enough to cover expenses?

• *Is the blog an effective sales funnel?* Similar to the income question, is the blog funneling traffic and potential buyers to the business, either online or offline? If not, the blog can become a financial drain.

• *Is the blog's topic lifespan limited?* Blogs that center around a specific news topic, event, or technology can have a limited lifespan. For example, writing a blog completely dedicated to a specific smartphone style or model will only be relevant as long as that model exists. It may have some historical value after the model is retired, but it will be unlikely to generate much news and blog post inspiration in the years ahead, giving it limited ROI (return on investment).

• *Is the blog topic trending steady or going upward?* Similar to a blog's topic lifespan just discussed, the topic's trending should be considered. Even if the topic has a long potential lifespan or is an "evergreen" topic, it may drop off in terms of interest over time as public interest or attitudes change. If topic interest is slipping, pumping significant investment into it may be counterproductive.

• *Is the blog's topic scalable?* Super niche topics might be able to be covered in a few blog posts. So is it worth launching and maintaining an entire blog to publish this information? Probably not. Might be better to publish as a subtopic or even as guest posts on a related blog.

The Case For and Against Dead Blogs

"Why not just leave the blog sit there? The information is still relevant and I might show up in a search."

Valid point! Indeed, the information presented on an inactive blog may be relevant for years. So there is a case to keep a blog open for that very reason, especially if some posts have had a lot of traffic and have been effective in the past. But the following need to be considered:

• **Cost.** If not using one of the free blog platforms, there will be costs to maintain the domains, hosting, etc., even if no one continues to post. Is it worth a few hundred dollars a year to keep that blog active? Are the sales leads or advertising revenue from an inactive blog enough to cover the costs of continuing to host it?

• **Image.** An old, never updated website or blog can send a negative "we don't care" message to blog visitors.

CHAPTER 11: DID I BURST YOUR BLOGGING BUBBLE?

I have to apologize if, after reading this, you feel kind of bummed about blogging. I really didn't mean to burst your bubble.

However, I'm guessing that you're glad you know what obstacles you might face. You might also be comforted when you realize that the challenges you're facing are not all your fault and that other bloggers are experiencing them, too.

Blogging for money is possible, just not probable, for many bloggers. Those that make a living at it rarely earn income from just the writing of it. They're usually experts at sales, marketing, public relations, social media, public speaking, ecommerce, and self publishing... in addition to being experts in their topic of interest.

I'm not trying to discourage you from blogging completely. But I am going to discourage you from being sucked into the fantasy of writing a blog as an easy way to riches. It is just another channel through which you connect with your fans or customers. I do hope that, by reading this eBook, you now can take a realistic look at your blog and turn it into something that is rewarding for both you and your audience.

All the best, *Heidi*

ABOUT HEIDI THORNE

I'm Dr. Heidi Thorne, MBA/DBA, a business nonfiction author and speaker. I specialize in helping authors and writers avoid embarrassing and expensive mistakes with their self published books and blogs. I've been an active blogger since 2010 and have self published several print books, eBooks, and audio books on small business, marketing, and self publishing. My podcast, *The Heidi Thorne Show*, discusses real world self publishing issues.

To learn more about me, visit my website at HeidiThorne.com.

www.ingramcontent.com/pod-product-compliance
Lightning Source LLC
Chambersburg PA
CBHW072242170526
45158CB00002BA/984